It's About Time.

Richard L. Ratliff
Illustration: Jason Ratliff

Copyright © 2013 Richard Ratliff
Illustrations by Jason Ratliff
All rights reserved.
ISBN: 1484833252
ISBN-13: 9781484833254

Dedicated to my lovely wife, Barbara, and my two wonderful children, Jennifer and Jason. Especially, Jason, whose artistic talents inspired me to write after a long time of silence. His art compliments the poems in this book and his work can be found at jasonratliff.net

There is a question that lingers: what is poetry? I describe poetry as "escaping through words to express that which is internal that is translated as feelings, thoughts, emotions as to be communicated externally. It flows from our lips through spoken word…it drips from our pens and pencils onto paper and notebooks so we can look back and reflect…it is art…it is remixed and spun through sound…like a love song or a rap verse never in reverse, never to be silenced as it is alive." [1] My appreciation for the written word began with classics such as Emily Dickinson, Jane Austen, and Edgar Allan Poe which led way for Langston Hughes, Zora Neale Hurston, Allen Ginsberg, Nikki Giovanni, Rita Dove, Sonia Sanchez and Maya Angelou to more contemporary works by Tupac Shakur, Saul Williams, Jill Scott, Jewel and Ashanti Douglas. Yes. I read and absorb their words that comfort and elevate me to form and write my own. And there is always a question of: are poets writers and how good are your poems if no one understands them but you? Interesting enough, I read poems written by others to feel, and so when I read "Neck Massage" by the author of this book, I felt each word as if it were a telescope peeking into my heart. Sigh. Rick has a subtle seductive approach to his writing that mentally wraps you with comfortable words.

In essence, poetry is art. Poetry is freedom of expression. Poetry is soft and velvet. Poetry is harsh and rough. Most important, poetry is raw. Poetry is real; it is seeing and feeling as one creates images that dance along a colorful storyline. Poetry is sexy and liquid kisses that taste of honey. Poetry is when one loves another yet they are too shy to speak so they release that tender and erotic splash of emotions which form poetry. Yes. I was thrilled to be introduced to Rick's work through our online writing community, and I sincerely admire his cool and effortless flow of masculine sensuality. I am humbled to be a part of Rick's publishing journey and am sure that every piece of his puzzle will fall into perfect place. Forward.

Kesha L Johnson-Clark is an indie writer, poet and spoken word artist.
Her books are available through: amazon.com/author/keshajohnsonclark

Source [1]from "Poetry Defined" http://www.poetfreak.com/text/119236/poetry-defined.html

Section 1:
LOST LOVES

I'll be damned T.S. ... 2

She is all of you ... 4

No. One ... 6

Parked ... 8

Neck massage ... 10

I remember ... 12

She is ... 14

Older woman ... 16

World's fair ... 18

My love swells ... 20

Time ... 22

Thoughts of Spain ... 24

Stolen time ... 26

I inhale you ... 28

Petals ... 30

Breathless conversation ... 32

Ten years after ... 34

Grand Canyon ... 36

I'm sorry ... 38

I love you ... 40

Section 2:
OTHER MUSINGS

Elephant ... 42

Zebra ... 44

Giraffe ... 46

Lamp post ... 48

I've seen Sinatra ... 50

Sticks and Stones ... 52

The River ... 54

Giants ... 56

Young Lion ... 58

Memories ... 60

I'LL BE DAMNED T.S.

I'll be damned if I need to roll up my pants
I'll wear socks with sandals and eat lobster claws:
No I'll rage rage against the dying of fashion laws

I have learned which way to pee out the car window

Time is passing : not leaden stepping
But sprinting on winged feet,
Quicksilver slipping by.
I'm tired, the smoky haze makes
Me want to run around the house curl up to be
Or not, as the river runs in Joycean fashion
Through the channels of my mind.

As the women come. And
Go basking in the afterglow

God is my superman,
I tug on his cape.
Like trying to peel a Concord grape
With my teeth, my tongue gets in the way.

Looking out the window while following
Cars with their windows down.
I try prophesying
What they too may have learned leastwise
I need new wipers for my eyes.

As the women come. And
Go basking in the afterglow

Will a Windsor knot be the answer?
Could I be just hanging around,
No I'll pass the cars just to be sure
My uncertainty doesn't my biography obscure.

The clock: It seems hand bound,
Or just the battery winding down
By the certainty or insanity of time.
Am I going to be an unfinished work in progress?
If I stay at the same address,
If I stand my ground.

As the women come. And
Go basking in the afterglow

Stand around get run over.
The clock hands never shake with me.
The morning provided grazing clover
And noon had pretentious lovers,
The evening gives way to stability
But the clock winds on to end the day.

So far from the beginning;
Loosening my under pinning.
Expectation of erection is only that.
Walk with uneven gait thinking
Of not falling, stopping- just resting.
I should go and go like Pheidippides

As the women come. And
Go basking in the afterglow

SHE
IS
ALL
OF
YOU

She is all of you, each of you, and only you

She lays sleeping,
Her breasts like pale, soft moon lit pillows.
The dim light, like milk, flows
down her taut stomach
Collecting in the little funnel that becomes a naval.
As the stars drip light into the night
I drink it in as the night slips away.
Like a sailor I navigate by the stars,
Like riding a wave surfing to the shore
Navigating the currents; the swells and waves.

It is a hot night,
As I lay now on the shore exposed,
the warm waters lap over me,
Like a barber's towel engulfing me

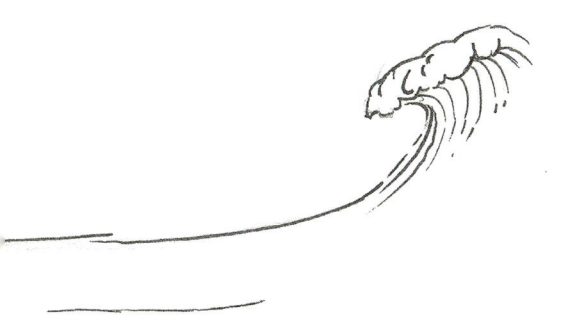

NO.
ONE

Bath powder on your breasts
That I caressed
You felt like silk

So surprisingly timid was I
Our first time. You so gently
Helped lead the way intently.
Did you hide your experience
While letting me seem victorious?

We parked so many places
We could have used a valet

Win Schuler's was class,
But mosquitoes in the Michigan woods,
They made love bites on my ass.
No room in the canoe even for that.

That house I hitchhiked down to,
A warm bed of your softness.
Football weekend at a brother's place; times too few
Where your scent lingers after you.

Memories are sometimes fleeting.
But not your first love
I cried after you... still needing

After ten years strong and vivid
After two decades still exquisite
After five they begin to fade
Just flashes here and there
A whiff of your scent somewhere
A lingering synaptic flash decayed

PARKED

Off on a side street
Away from the bright light.
Making love in the front seat,
Fumbling with the buttons
Straps and hooks at night.
Steaming up the window pane
While hoping to be discreet.
Steering wheel wasn't enough to constrain
Passion we could not contain
Good thing they weren't bucket seats

NECK MASSAGE

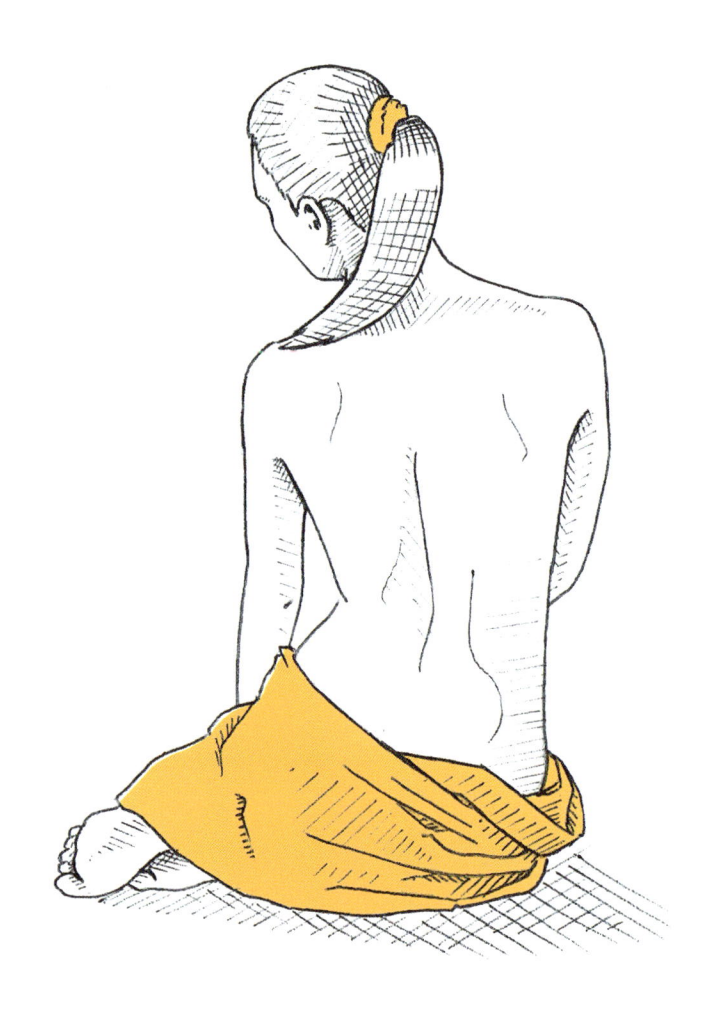

My hands knead the day
From your tense shoulders
Your back and sides I manipulate my way
Down to the bottom of your spine
So soft so warm
You allow only so much of mine
Your shell of protection up
Your desires in check
What fear have you assigned
That cloaks you from me
Let fall away the veil around your neck

I
Remember

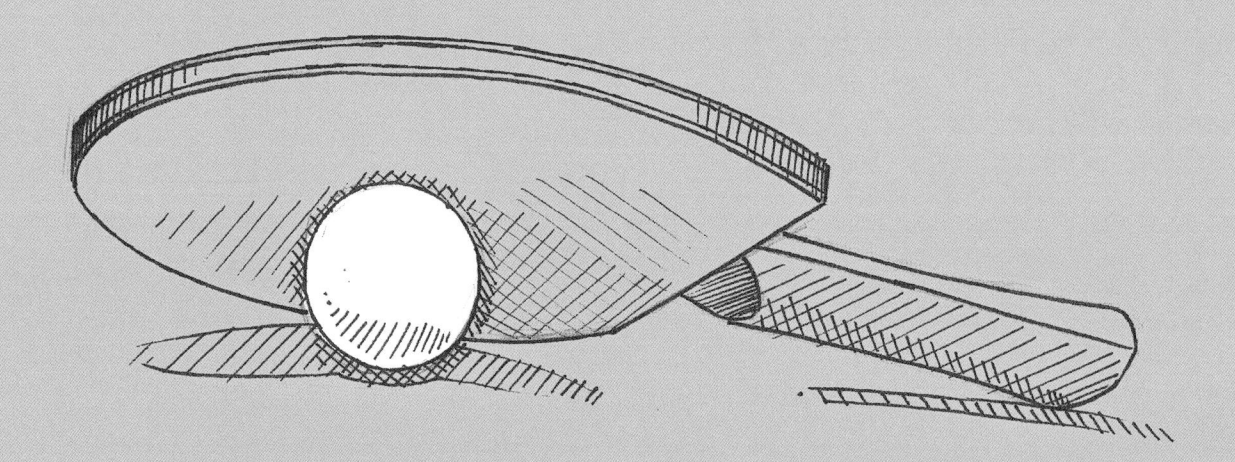

I remember your silky softness,
My arm around your waist;
Hand on your hip graced
By the thought of your embrace.

Your rosy lips so beguiling.
The eyes wow your eyes blue lasers,
Exploding blue sapphires.
They always conspire to inspire.

Your voice could be Jackie Kennedy,
So softly innocent and pure.
Elegantly simple honesty,
That brought out my chivalry.

So gently intense you foam
And shave my face beard stubble.
Only you would allow
The peace sign to mean victory
If my team won.

One night in a no tell motel,
We were Clinton chaste.
It's been so long since I was
Ray Robertson that out dad chased.

If my feet smell would you shower with me this time?

Frat parties, proms and fashion shows,
Red retrievers on escalators,
Hemming skirts up like elevators.
That old Chevy with the top down,
Sport coat to the movies downtown
Where did we park that night?
Ping pong in the basement right?

Why didn't you go to Spain
Avoiding the rain or possible pain?
Could have been our opportunity
Would we have a blue eyed majorette.
Dressed in red and black?

Not a stream, no: white water rapids of conciseness
Connected by bicycles to Chevys
To Mercedes

SHE IS

She is supple and soft
Slowly quick and taut
She is here - yet not
Elusive and still to touch
To touch - yet not
She is intertwined and uncaught
Expressive and quiet
She is opaque and dark
Earthen yet a lark
She is a smile in the dark

OLDER WOMAN

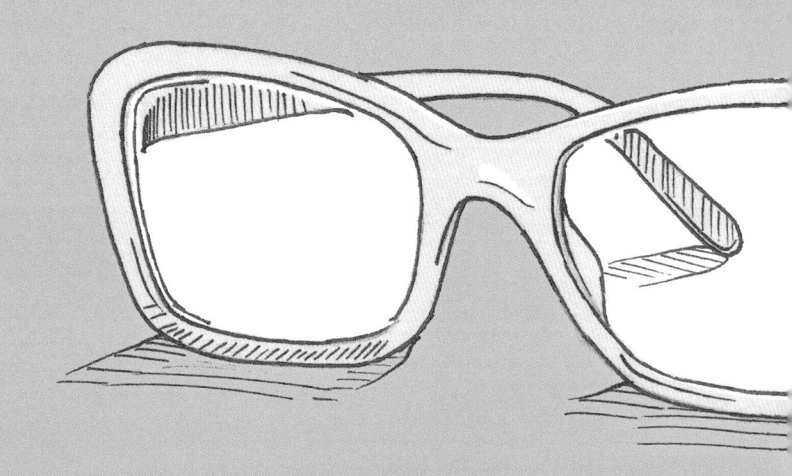

I didn't know until later,
You fooled me with your guile.
I was twenty you were thirty,
Ten years didn't seem to matter.
Was it the glasses that made you look so wide eyed,
The child like smile,
Or just your youthful chatter.
I think the latter.

A mature romance long planned,
I was a short term diversion,
Always moving up were you.
No breathless clawing,
Just an experienced mounting of the trophy.
Parking at your age, you were cute
And ravenous.

Going from laborer to artist to politician.
No effect on your ambition,
You married up again
And moved on with no inhibition

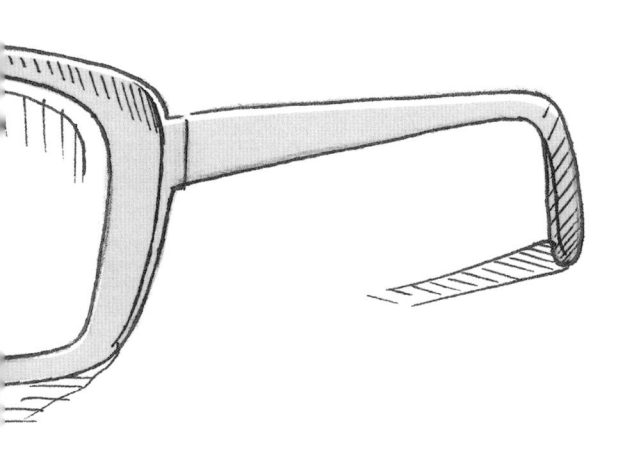

page 17

WORLD'S FAIR

World's Fair just for us two.
So long to travel for the first time.
Three piece suit and you,
Walking between nations
Pretending to be grownup.
Returning in a fog from there to expectations.

The home town motel bed we messed
That time of the month.
I blessed your breast
With kisses as
We celebrated your in laws script.

The wall at school, peeing in a coke bottle.
Naked to the world,
Or was it a beer bottle?

Give the ball to Leroy,
Meet at Arnie's or the Chocolate Shop?
Run for homecoming queen while coming in Canada.

Christmas in the basement:
Mom almost catching us entwined
We could have been out on the pavement
What would have been the payment?

Rubbing the carpet in my apartment.
Your nipples hard as a pencil eraser.
You were my treasure;
I was lost in you that time like no other.
There is no replacement.

Teach to appreciate scotch,
And now it is an old fashioned
Or a rusty nail

Embrace in Orlando,
Times past faint afterglow

page 19

MY LOVE SWELLS

My love swells for you.
Erect and proud.
Can I convince you to envelop me?

Guide me along, point the way,
And be gentle.
The kegel has given you such power.

You have so enthralled me;
I feel I must possess you,
But it is you who weaves the magic
And squeezes out my love

page 21

TIME

Too bad there was no stop watch on us,
No way to stay young no way
For time to be frozen:
Woven into emotion without erosion
As the lovers on Keats urn caress,
Let sad eyes see again and begin
To absorb your beauty once more.
To fill the urn with the wine of all time
And taste your flower once more

THOUGHTS OF SPAIN

Bright red lipstick,
Earthen at my request.
Changed out of your cocoon,
So lovely undressed.
You were soft and lithe,
With lovely velvet breasts
(A foreboding of distress).

Tried to remember: put the seat down
So the roommate wouldn't frown.
Warmed the bed for both of us,
Warm and penetrating.
Long and slender with a lovely navel
And eyes so hazel.

Come with me to Spain and be my love
A chance vacation I can afford
For a long distance date explored

Slim trim supple and pragmatic
With beautiful playful eyes.
An ample lover of Victoria Beer;
Made love on Costa Del Sol.
Was I too cavalier?

Saw a bull fight from the stands.
Crossed the straights of Gibraltar.
Splashed by the Mediterranean.

Went to Africa, Morocco, and Tangier.
Saw the snake charmers at the bazaar.
Thought you were so creative,
Riding on a camel like a native.

So loving and lovely were you;
I'm sorry my mind let go so soon,
Too quick one afternoon.

Saw you at a wedding
So beaming bright for the future
I'm so sorry we lost you to the fear you were dreading

STOLEN TIME

Hours here, a long day, a night
A weekend of need.
All seeking to reclaim past times,
And we seemed to succeed
For a very very long time; sometimes.

Flowing like melted butter.
Will you hug me in the shower,
Or the oversized tub,
Can I come out now?

You teach and move me,
Coupled together entwined.
Dark blue sapphire trinkets,
And ruddy birthmarks.

Running out of the precipitation,
Your hook and I popping open.
A suddenly exposed flirtation,
We let it all happen,
I can come out now!

Never made breakfast.
Had apple pie for lunch.
Jane and Margo all made up participants,
You could always antique.
Tasty's eatable arrangements,
Strawberries and whipped cream;
Some things are a recurring theme

I
INHALE
YOU

I inhale you, I envelop and explore you,
I digest the fluids of the night.
I love our coupled thoughts of words and deeds and wants and needs

Growing in my mind.
Been and to be
Our days and ways of yesterday

Hungrily listening to your thigh,
Moist creases of your inguen.
Not hearing a one act monologue,
But a humid conversation

I am Calais viewing the White Cliffs of Dover

My tongue penetrates your lips
A kind of tongue wrestling match

Your breasts are soft ripe peaches.
You gently open to me and moistly
Close around my infatuation.
I try to dominate but your creation
Traps and encloses me.
Slowly I try to postpone, but finality is quickly coming

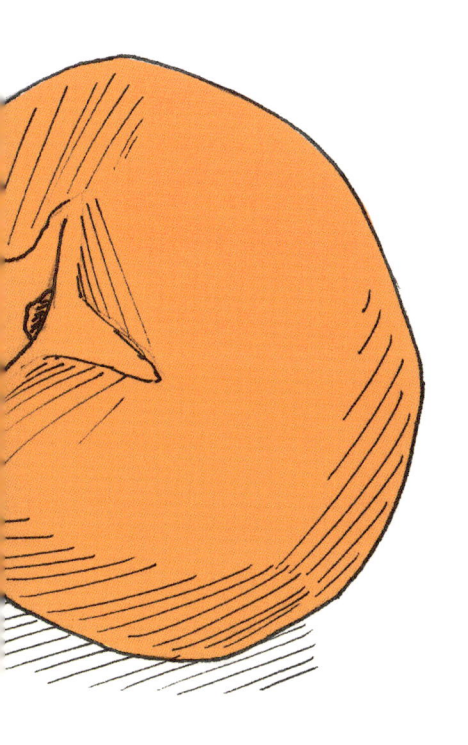

PETALS

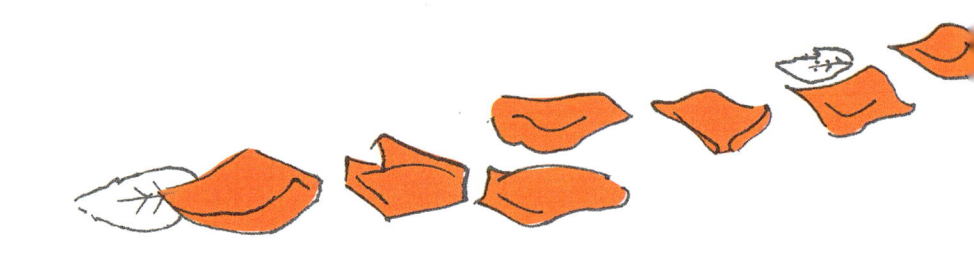

A surprise for you at the door
Petals on the floor,
A path of colored blossoms leading to the nights affair.
All the thorns are gone, stripped bare.
Red yellow white and lavender.
The fragrance flows up like a warm blanket
As it spreads across the room and fills her head.
Luring a big breasted woman to my bed.
No need for robes or lace,
Leave them on the floor folded in place.
You cannot hide in the dark beneath the sheets
You are in full bloom even in pale light
Your blossom unfurled and wide eyed.
Innocently enticing, if that can be tonight

BREATH-LESS CONVERS-ATION

Oh do me --again

(You overwhelm me)

Again and again

(I can't keep up)

Coming again and split asunder

(I am too soft for now ---wait)

Can't wait --come here!

You own the wet spot

(Let me repose a while)

Hurry while I'm here and now
A visible slit in time

Remember the batteries
Shake and bake

(And let me rest my factories)

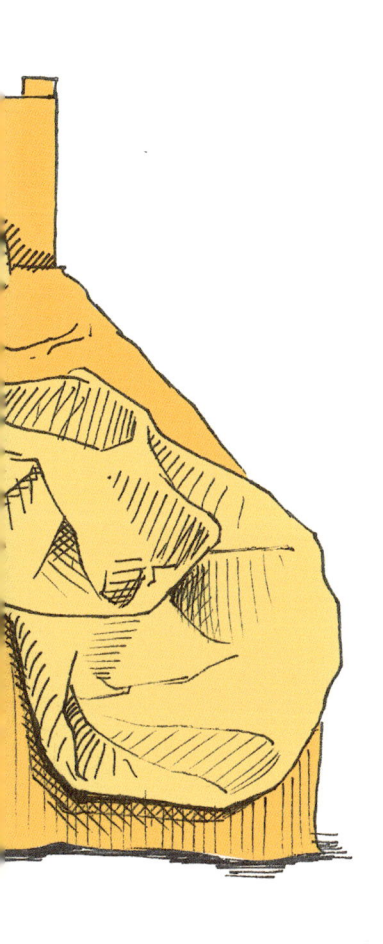

page 33

TEN YEARS AFTER

Ten Years After really was a play,
For you anyway

You were a wild turkey
Starting on our journey

Couldn't fly but could
Make memories for history
Reverie for most half a century

All that has gone and will go by
Is connected to you in many ways,
Misunderstood for so many days

You always are there
When I crashed you let me prove myself.
Yes you softly care for me
With unforeseen strength
In silent bitterness to fate,
Even as I am a silly repartee

I really wish we could hug
How did we lose that?
Did we agree to disagree and shrug?

Time has made us silent lovers.
We are partners of silence.
Just seeming to be a continuing habit.
We made it all these years,
We should hug again

GRAND CANYON

Like mother earth's legs spread
Leading to the source.
Thighs flexed and taught,
Muscular, tan and coursed
With shades of the event
Somehow having relent
To the coming climax of
The river running through...

I'M SORRY

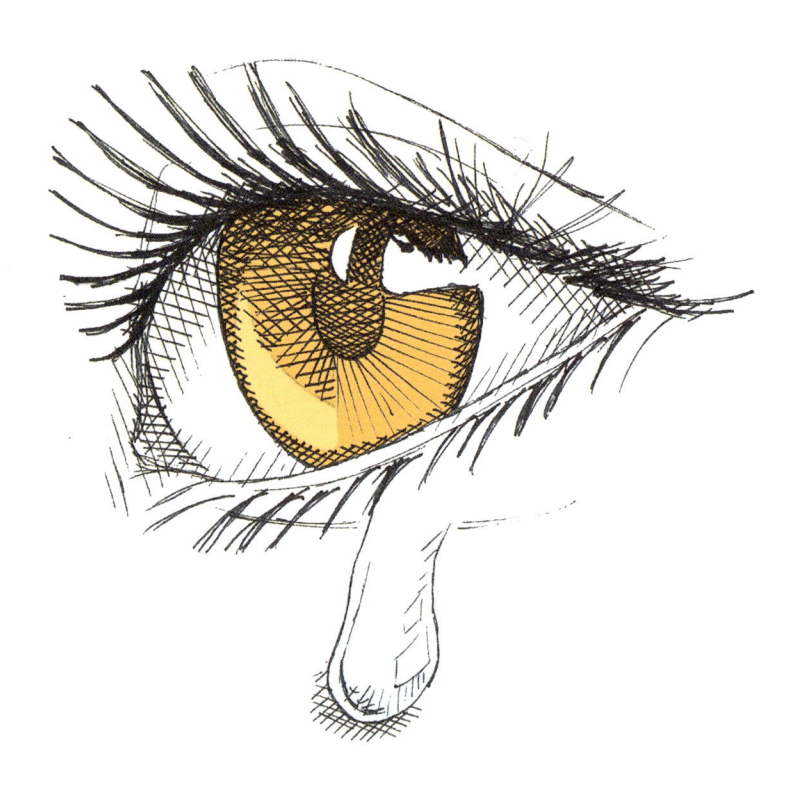

I'm sorry I couldn't be
What you wanted us to be.
Was it all pretend?
Did it portend
This state of withdrawal.
Was it only years of kisses
In the dark?
Unable to see each other.
I thought I saw into you.
Were my eyes straining too much?
I thought we touched each other,
And we really did uncover such

There are places in my mind
I like to go and
Rather than depressed thoughts
I find you there

page 39

I
LOVE
YOU

I love you,
For all these years I knew
I haven't said it enough.
There have been more than a few loves in my life;
They all have left a mark on my heart,
Yet they all depart

But only you were the love of my life,
Only you have been my wife.
You have shared my bed,
And my heart for all these years.
A partner in this life's puzzle

Our life has been a journey,
A mixing of our chemistry.
You are the bed rock of the family.
I should have gotten the milk

How well I remember,
The shore line being swallowed by the sea,
Your dress swaying on the cabin door,
Watching our children being born,
And all the love I had for you.
It was a piece of cake.

I remember funny trips to theme parks
Sleeping on the little bed at your parents,
Trying to help you grieve when they were gone.
All part of the riddle of our life

page 41

ELEPHANT

You always eat an elephant
One bite at a time!
A super-sized meal to remember.
To circumnavigate the perimeter
Pay attention or you'll get lost at the starting gate.
Use the horn to communicate.
Afraid of that mouse,
Can't jump or really run
But I can blow my own horn,
And stomp and shake things up

ZEBRA

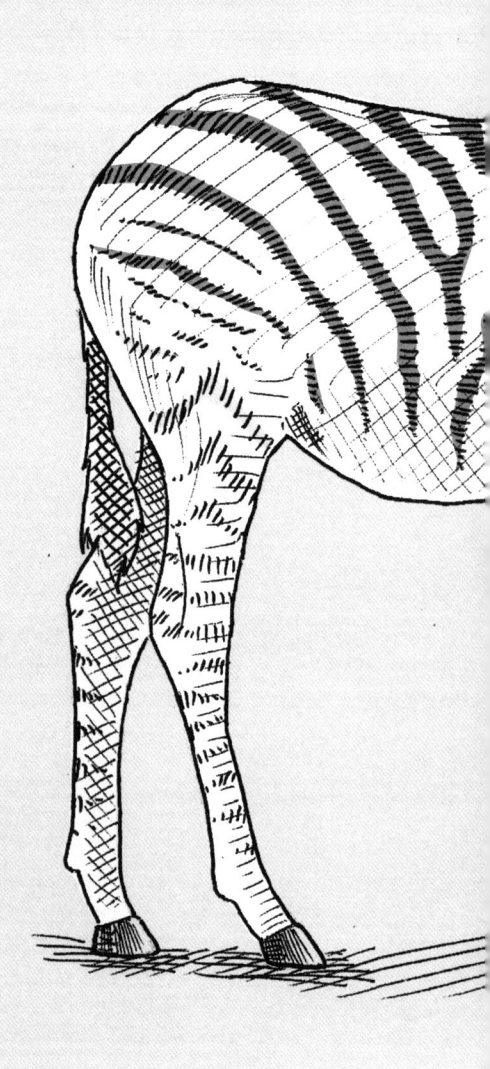

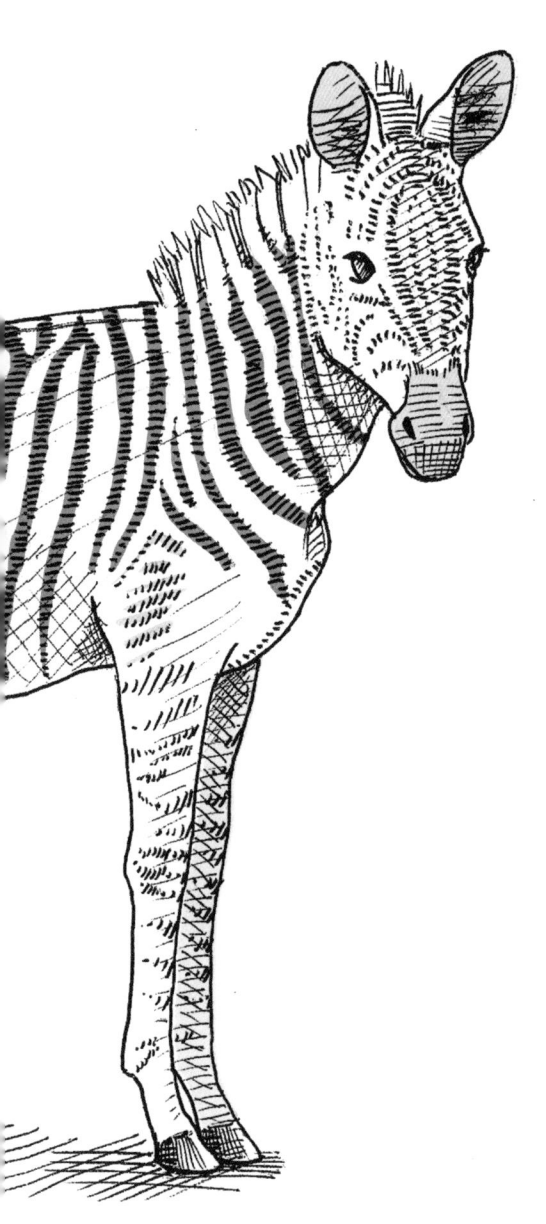

Black and white camouflage,
Or just a suit you have to wear?
Are you jailed in this jungle
Are all the lines zippers holding you together?
Where did you get those long argyle socks,
Is that a painted smile striped on your face?
Like that Mohawk: Mr. T would be proud

GIRAFFE

Head in the sky,
Feet on the ground.
When you and your friends gather,
It's a new kind of high five.
Do you and your girlfriend neck a lot?
How have you found
The weather up there so high?
You need such a very long scarf tied in a knot.

page 47

LAMP
POST

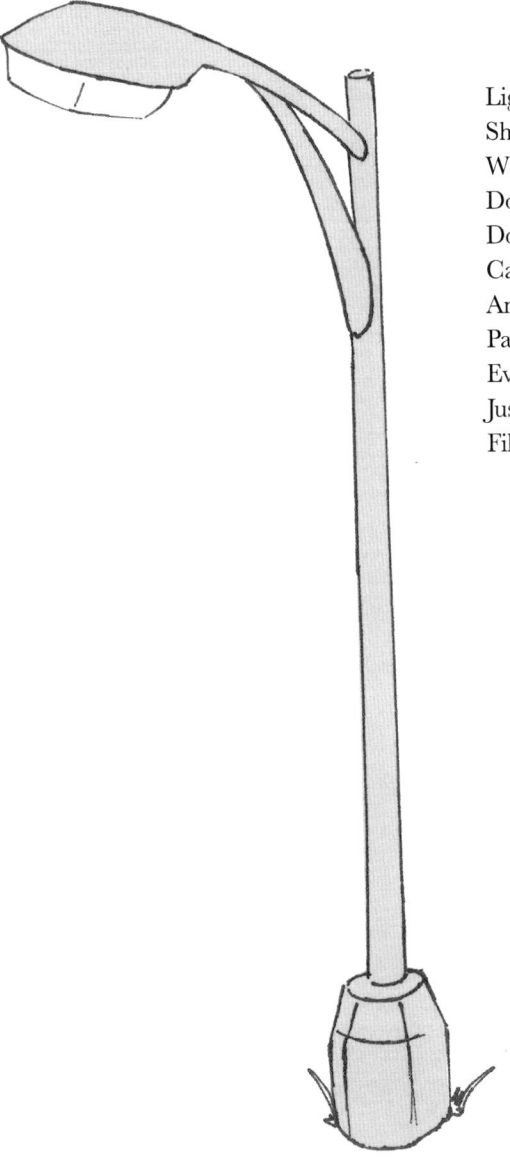

Light at dusk from a lamp post
Shining on an empty bench.
Who did it host?
Do their thoughts and deeds sit and linger?
Does each separate incandescent flicker
Cast a different colored shadow with its finger,
And write its ghost upon the pavement.
Past history for us to consider
Even though there is nothing there,
Just a remaining colored fragment
Filaments of times past affair

I'VE SEEN SINATRA

I've seen Sinatra I've seen Elvis,
Both live on stage,
I've been to both sides now.
Saw Ricky Nelson live at my age
Johnny Mathis and Paul Anka too,
Helped remember lost loves pages.
Nancy Wilson entertained my heart,
Maynard Ferguson opened the register,
Peter Paul and Mary played to the dragon:
Tilted so as not to fall off the wings.
What a Magical mystery life sings

STICKS & STONES

Sticks and stones, roof shingles,
Doors with ruler marks up the edge,
Not a place for singles.
Scratches on the table ledge,
The ghost of the little dogs.
When you build a house
You nail down memories,
Paint and stain the fabric of time

Six foot trees grown to forty,
A cedar deck a hand dug pond,
The family desk too big to keep.
Little things in the drawers,
Just junk but junk with memories so fond

Downsizing is sad,
Admitting September is coming.
No more room for the big chair with the worn cushion,
The books with dog eared pages too many for moving

The bedrooms that grew too old for
Children no more.
The ornamented trees so many;
Too many to remember.
All the decades of gifts in the great room
Shared with parents long gone.

That big kitchen table,
So many holiday turkeys and hams.
A time for the wedding tableware.
What kind of container do you use for memories?
How do you pack up a door or trees?

Tell me how to downsize life's histories

THE RIVER

I flow from the narrows as a stream.
At the source: fast flowing fresh and clear
And gather size and strength as I go near.
Rubbing nutrients from the bed and the shore,
Getting strong enough for those to
Ride the wave and enjoy my strong flow.
Creating commerce and family as I go.

The boats of life ride me from their tributaries.
Tributaries flow to me, like branches of a tree.
The grooves in the shore vibrate the song of the river.
Creating commerce and family as they go.

I am that river that source I am the aorta,
Pulsing thru the landscape.
Arteries flow and branch letting life escape.
Creating commerce and family as they go.

Yet as I expand I slow until
Reaching the salty tears of the great expanse.
Hopefully I have brought those along to safety
Before I disappear.
Creating commerce and family where they dock

GIANTS

No mater how hard we try,
We steal from giants by and by.
A phrase, a meter, an image we imply.
The raven slips in when talking shadows,
Or the frosty fork in the road,
Or Walt's song of me to decode.
We do it without knowing,
And when we know we're owing
We expect others to understand;
It is a reference - nothing more

They are part of us.
We are not islands.
We know how cruel April is.
You only pick cherries in the summer?
If the lease is paid.
The lover in me thinks not
Even Ferlinghetti but the only rhyme is spaghetti

YOUNG LION

He is the young lion of my pride,
Learning and growing, stretching and exceeding.
Looking up and even above a mane astride,
Having measured himself beside,
Always looking at the preceding.

Lions seek to leave a scent - a mark.
And I have struggled to leave mine.
Clawing marks upon my life and time.
Struggling to ascend and accumulate,
As if by towering to reach the mark.

He is my mark,
Not that she is less,
Just that sons and fathers
Are like mirrors and daughters are soft.

It is a way to know you have not been playing solitaire

page 59

MEMORIES

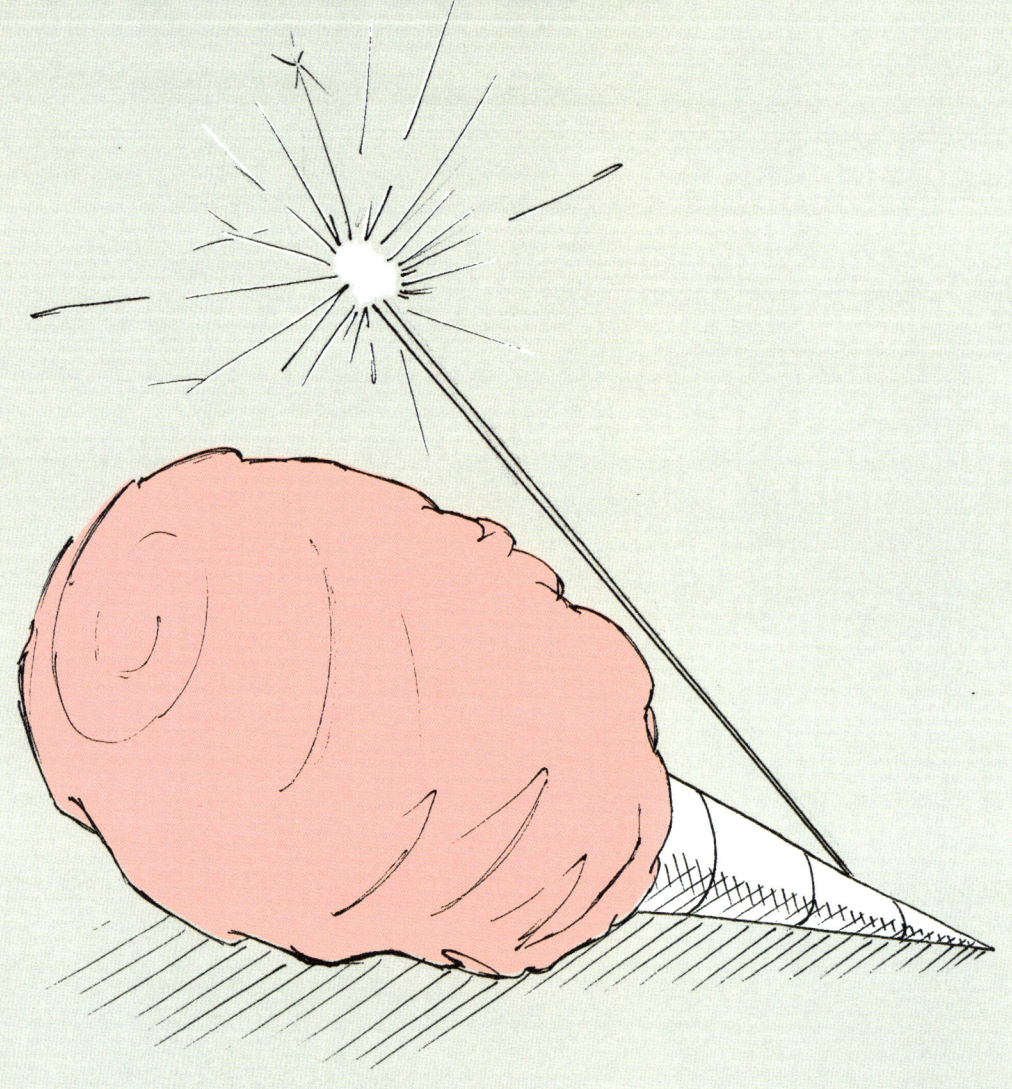

MEMORIES
Are solid when you bump into them

The smell of soft memories
Like shadowy wisps of cotton candy.
So sweet; yet fleeting hollow calories
Until bumping into them gives realization
A solid feelings of fancy.
Like the fingers of my mind grasping
In the shadows of realities,
Forming new directions; new memories to compare
With those long ago and so fair.

Be careful while rummaging through the recesses of your mind
When all you are looking for is a memory's hand to hold.
For sometimes in the dark
You can run into a spark
That jolts and flashes thoughts across your mind,
Blinded by the sparks of the past
While trying to squeeze the future

Made in the USA
Lexington, KY
14 April 2015